Leaf & Tree

GUIDE

BY RONA BEAME
Illustrations by Kimble Mead

Workman Publishing • New York

For all my wonderful children,
Julia, David, Richard,
Andrew, and Sara,
and for my dear friends
Richard Rosen and Neila Fisher,
who make me laugh.

Published simultaneously in Canada by Thomas Allen
& Son Limited.

Library of Congress Cataloging-in-Publication Data
available upon request.

ISBN: 0-7611-3319-4

Workman books are available at special discounts
when purchased in bulk for premiums and sales pro-
motions as well as for fund-raising or educational use.
Special editions or book excerpts can also be created
to specification. For details, contact the Special Sales
Director at the address below.

Photo Credits pages 56–71: All images Dorling
Kindersley, Ltd., except page 63, middle: Herman,
D.E./USDA NRCS, and page 71, middle: Larry
Allain/USGS NWRC.

Workman Publishing Company, Inc.
708 Broadway
New York, New York 10003-9555
www.workman.com

Printed in China

First printing: April 2004
10 9 8 7 6 5 4 3 2 1

Acknowledgments

For all their help, I would like to thank: Doreen Rosen, Joe Beitel, Jeannie Fernsworth, Lothian Lynas, and Mike Ruggiero at the New York Botanical Garden; Ken Finch and Richard Haley at the New Canaan Nature Center in Connecticut; and the Chappaqua Library.

Contents

Introduction 6

Part I
The Great
Leaf Hunt 11

Part II
All About Trees
and Leaves 37

Part III
Some Common Trees (And How to Tell Them Apart) *55*

Part IV
Projects *73*

Introduction

Investigating Trees

Have you ever brought home a leaf and wondered what kind of tree it belonged to?

Have you ever saved a pinecone because you liked the way it felt and wondered what was inside?

Have you ever wanted to know what causes those strange bumps you sometimes see on leaves?

Then get set to go on an exciting nature hunt! In the woods and parks, on the city streets—in your own backyard—you'll track down and identify dozens of leaves, seeds, and cones as you investigate the wonderful world of trees.

You'll become a backyard explorer, and backyard explorers are special people. They are curious. They like to collect things. They like to solve nature's mysteries. They like to have fun.

Whenever backyard explorers go outside, they look around and see what's going on in the trees and on the ground. Have the buds opened yet? Are there flowers or fruit on the twigs? Are the trees raining seeds? What kind of nuts is that squirrel hoarding for winter?

Winter, spring, summer, or fall, once you're a backyard explorer, there's always something to do outdoors.

The Backyard Explorer Kit

You're about to go on a hunt for leaves. How will you know what you're looking for? Your Backyard Explorer Kit will make your adventures in the great outdoors fun and easy. It will help you understand how trees grow, learn easy tricks to identify the trees around you, and master projects you and your friends will enjoy all year.

It includes descriptions of leaves, seeds, nuts, cones, pods, and berries for you to find. It fits easily in your pocket. Later, you can read more about the many kinds of trees that live with us in our backyards.

You'll also take your plastic Leaf Collecting Envelope to protect your tree treasures until you get them home.

The Leaf Collecting Album contains twenty-five sturdy cards for matching, saving, and displaying the best of your collection.

We'll tell you all about how to press and mount your finds, and lots of fun things to do with the outdoors—when you're indoors! (See pages 73–96.)

So let's go, explorers, on the Great Leaf Hunt . . .

THE EXPLORER'S CODE

You will not hurt a tree if you take leaves from it, but do it very carefully. Keep these commonsense rules in mind when exploring outdoors.

- Never peel bark from a tree. Trees need their bark, just like people need their skin.

- Never pick anything from a neighbor's tree without asking permission.

- Never pick anything when you are exploring a nature preserve.

- Never break off a branch or twig.

- Never eat any fruit, berry, leaf, or flower unless you check it out with your parents. It could be poisonous.

- Trees are alive, just like us! Never do anything to hurt them.

PART I

The Great Leaf Hunt

Explore and Find

O kay, explorers. It's a perfect day for a leaf hunt. You'll need this book and the Leaf Collecting Envelope. Also, put a damp rag or paper towel in the envelope to keep leaves from drying out too fast and curling up.

Leaf Shapes

Believe it or not, you're going to identify leaves just as a botanist (scientist who studies plants) does, based on the way they grow, their edges, and whether they have lobes. Here are the main types you'll be looking for:

Smooth-Edged Simple Leaf

Toothed Simple Leaf

 Hand-Shaped
Simple Leaf

 Hand-Shaped
Compound Leaf

 Feather-Shaped
Simple Leaf

 Feather-Shaped
Compound Leaf

 Cluster Needles

 Single Needles

 Scaly Leaves

HOW LEAVES GROW

Leaves may seem to be sprouting from a tree without rhyme or reason, but all deciduous leaves either grow opposite one another or in an alternating pattern.

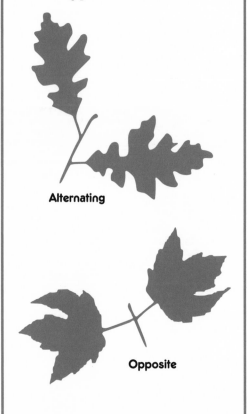

Alternating

Opposite

All deciduous leaves are also either simple or compound.

A simple leaf is all one piece, while a compound leaf is divided into separate leaflets, all attached to the same leaf stem.

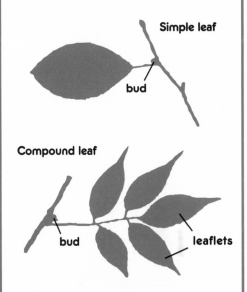

Simple leaf

bud

Compound leaf

bud

leaflets

How can you tell the difference between a leaf and a leaflet? Look at where the leaf and its stem join the twig. If there is a bud, it's a leaf. Buds only grow where the stem of a whole leaf joins the twig. If you don't see a bud, you are looking at a leaflet from a compound leaf.

An average tree removes ten pounds of pollutants from the air each year.

If the leaflets grow on each side of the main stem, they are called pinnate. If the main stem has little stems on each side, and the leaflets are attached to those little stems, the leaves are called bipinnate.

(FIND)
Smooth-Edged Simple Leaf

Look for: A leaf that has a smooth edge. Run your finger around it. You shouldn't feel any bumps or teeth. Try to find different shapes: oval, heart-shaped, skinny, and long.

SUPER EXPLORERS

★ Botanists categorize leaves partly by their width. See where the leaves you collect are fattest—at the top, bottom, or middle. If you're not sure, bend the leaf in half to find out.

 (FIND)

Toothed Simple Leaf

Look for: A leaf that has toothed or jagged edges similar to the teeth on a saw. Toothed leaves can be any shape. They are the most common leaves.

Most have teeth that are easy to spot. Others have tiny teeth that you must look closely to see.

SUPER EXPLORERS

⭐ Look for leaves that have groups of little teeth between each of the big teeth.

(FIND)

Hand-Shaped Simple Leaf

Look for: A leaf shaped like your hand with its fingers spread. The main veins begin at the stem and run out at angles into the lobes.

Hand-shaped leaves can have two lobes or more. Some have lobes like long fingers. Other leaves have shorter lobes.

SUPER EXPLORERS

★ Like human fingerprints, no two leaves are exactly the same. It is easy to spot the differences in hand-shaped leaves: Take some leaves from the same tree, lay them on top of one another, and compare.

(FIND)

Hand-Shaped Compound Leaf

Look for: A leaf that looks like the hand-shaped simple leaf, but its lobes are cut into separate leaflets. They all radiate from one point, the way fingers spread out on a hand.

To tell a leaf from a leaflet, look at where the leaf joins the twig. Remember that a bud will grow only where the main stem of the whole leaf meets the twig. So if you see a bud at the base of a leaf, it's a leaf. If not, it's a leaflet.

Hand-shaped compound leaves may have three or more leaflets. The three-leaflet compound leaf is the most rare.

(FIND)

Feather-Shaped Simple Leaf

Look for: A leaf that looks something like a jagged feather. It has a long main vein that goes from the stem to the tip. On each side of this vein, opposite each other, are the feathery lobes. This type of leaf grows on oak trees.

Some oak leaves have rounded lobes; some have pointy lobes.

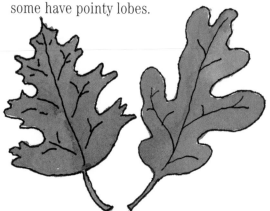

SUPER EXPLORERS

⭐ The leaves of the shingle oak, the laurel oak, the willow oak, and the live oak don't have lobes. See how many different oak leaves you can find.

Explorer's Tip: All oak trees have acorns. When you're searching for oak leaves, look for acorns under a tree.

(FIND)

Feather-Shaped Compound Leaf

Look for: A leaf that resembles a feather and is divided into leaflets growing opposite each other along a central stem. Remember to find the bud on the twig—then you will know if you are looking at a leaf or a leaflet.

Some feather-shaped compound leaves have hundreds of small leaflets. If the leaflets grow on each side of the main stem, they are called pinnate. If the main stem has little stems on each side, and the leaflets are attached to those little stems, the leaves are called bipinnate.

Can you find both kinds?

(FIND)

Alternate and Opposite Leaves

Look for: The way leaves are arranged on the twig. On some broadleaf trees, the leaves grow opposite each other on the twig. On others, they grow in alternate places along the twig.

Can you find both kinds?

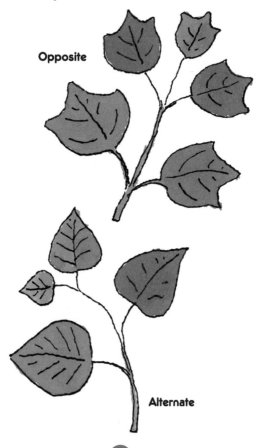

Opposite

Alternate

(FIND)

Palm Leaf

Palm leaves can be either feather-shaped or fan-shaped.

Can you find one?

Note: This hunt is only for explorers who live in warm climates, such as Florida, or who are lucky enough to vacation there. (But if you live in a state with cold winters, maybe you know someone who has an indoor palm.)

Coconuts are very heavy seeds, but there is enough air in a coconut's shell for it to float on water. When a coconut falls off a tree growing on a beach, it can roll down to the water and float away, ending up on other islands, sometimes hundreds of miles away.

(FIND)

Cluster Needles

Look for: An evergreen tree with long needles that grow in bunches, or clusters. Each cluster grows from one place on the twig.

Pine needles may grow in clusters of two, three, or five needles.

In El Valle, Panama, is a place called the Valley of Square Trees. All the trees have rectangular trunks. And no one can explain why.

(FIND)

Single Needles

Look for: An evergreen tree that has short, stiff needles. Each needle grows from its own place on the twig, like the teeth on a comb. Most are no more than an inch long.

Some single needles grow opposite each other on the twig. Others grow all around the twig.

SUPER EXPLORERS

⭐ You will need keen eyes to find a single needle with four sides and a sharp, pointy tip. See if you can also find a needle with a rounded tip.

(FIND)

Scaly Leaves

Look for: An evergreen tree with leaves that are tiny, overlapping scales like the petals on a rosebud. You have to look closely to see the scales because they are only an eighth of an inch long at most. The scales are so close together that they hide the twigs underneath.

Some scaly leaves look like lacy ferns. Other scaly leaves branch in all directions and are often prickly.

Note: Wear gloves or use a piece of paper towel when you pick twigs with sharp needles.

> The heaviest living tree is a sequoia named General Sherman. It weighs more than two million pounds—as much as 260 elephants.

(FIND)

Ginkgo (Maidenhair) Leaf

Look for: A leaf that looks like a duck's foot or a fan. The edges of the ginkgo leaf are wavy and many have a small V-shaped wedge cut out. Notice how long the stem is. Look for the ginkgo on city streets. And in the fall, female ginkgos drop stinky fruits, which supposedly make delicious soup (but please, don't pick them up off the street).

THE GINKGO TREE

Ginkgo trees (also known as maidenhair trees) have cones like conifers and broad leaves like most deciduous trees, but they don't belong to either group. They are the only survivors of a family of trees that were alive almost 200 million years ago—when dinosaurs were stomping through ancient forests!

(FIND)

Leaves Attacked by Insects

The best time to search for these leaves is in the late summer and autumn.

Look for: *The Swiss-cheese leaf.* Caterpillars and leaf beetles have made a good dinner of these leaves. Sometimes, there are more holes than leaf!

Look for: *The skeleton leaf.* This leaf is so eaten away by insects that there is practically nothing left—just veins and a stem.

Look for: *The gall leaf.* This leaf has strange bumps, of varying shapes, sizes, and colors, which may be hairy, sticky, or smooth. The bumps are galls, or insect homes, made by gall wasps and gall flies.

Oak leaves are some of the best places for finding galls. You might even find several different kinds on one leaf. Put the flattest galls on your Leaf Album card and save the rest for a gall project (see page 88).

Look for: *A leaf miner's leaf.* Leaf miners are tiny insects that live between the top and bottom layers of leaves. They begin their lives as eggs laid on the outside of a leaf. When they hatch, each leaf miner burrows its way inside the leaf and spends its youth alone, tunneling through the leaf tissue and eating as it goes.

Look carefully and you'll observe that the leaf miner's tunnel is very narrow at one end and wider at the other. That's because the insect gets fatter as it eats and tunnels along!

See if you can find a tiny exit hole at the wider end of the tunnel—most leaf miners leave the tunnel when they become adults.

All day long, a leaf breathes in carbon dioxide and breathes out oxygen and water vapor. This process of water evaporating from the leaves is called transpiration. It cools the leaves as well as the air surrounding a tree.

LOOK FOR BEAUTIFUL AUTUMN LEAVES

This hunt is for explorers who live in cold climates where the leaves turn color in autumn. Look for red, purple, orange, and yellow leaves, and some that have more than one, two, or even three colors. Try to find as many beautiful and unusual leaves as possible.

Notice that autumn leaves are tougher and stiffer than the delicate, soft leaves of spring. That's because autumn leaves are dry, whereas spring leaves are filled with water.

(FIND)

Surprise Packages

Trees produce lots of things you can collect and study besides leaves. Track down all the cones, pods, nuts, berries, and seeds you can find—and collect extras for projects.

Pods can look like stringbeans or pea pods hanging from branches. Pods get hard and leathery when they ripen, then split open to release their bean-shaped seeds.

Winged "seeds": Many seeds are housed in fruits that look like papery wings. Often they grow on the biggest trees, high up where they can catch the strongest breezes. When the seeds within the fruits are ripe, they fall off the tree. Their wings spin round and round, slowing their fall so they can stay up in the air and giving the wind a chance to carry them farther away from the parent tree. Look for winged seeds in the spring and fall.

Fluffy seeds are even lighter than winged seeds. When they escape from their fruits, fluffy seeds are attached to fine white, cottony hairs that help them sail through the air. Riding the winds, they can travel for miles. On some summer days, the air is filled with them—it seems like it's snowing!

The seed of a cottonwood tree can stay aloft longer than any other. A tiny seed surrounded by fluffy white hairs, it can fly for days.

Brown balls: Many trees grow fruit that are round, brown balls. These are seed capsules. Some balls stay on trees through the winter and release their seed in spring.

Acorns grow on oak trees all over the world. There are at least fifty different kinds of oaks in North America. Their acorns come in many

different shapes—but they always have a scaly cup at the base.

Spiny-husked nuts have either sharp thorns like a porcupine or spikes that look like cleats.

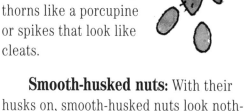

Smooth-husked nuts: With their husks on, smooth-husked nuts look nothing like the nuts we buy in the store. Instead, they resemble little limes dangling from trees.

Only when you take their husks off do you find the shell, like the wrinkled walnut or smooth pecan, that we commonly see.

Note: Walnut husks can dye hands brownish black.

Cones: Cones grow on most evergreen trees. At first they are soft and green, but after their seeds ripen they turn brown and become woody. It may take several years for the seeds inside to ripen. There are two winged seeds on each scale of most cones. When a cone's seeds are ripe, its

scales open so the seeds can fly away. Unlike the fruit of broadleaf trees, some cones stay on the trees long after their seeds have gone. Most of the open cones you find on the ground do not have seeds inside.

Berry-cones are found on many junipers and cedars. They look like blue berries but they are really tiny blue cones. If you look very closely, you will see the over-lapping scales.

THE DEADLIEST TREE

The manchineel grows in Florida's Everglades and on Caribbean beaches. Every part of the tree is poisonous—the bark, leaves, sap, and fruit. If the tree sap touches your skin, it causes blisters. If the sap gets into your eyes, it can blind you. The fruit looks like a small green or yellow apple. It even smells like an apple, but just one bite causes terrible pain or death. The only creature that can eat the fruit and live is a local land crab.

FLESHY AND DRY FRUITS

A tree's fruit is the part that protects the seeds. Everyone knows that apples and oranges are fruits. These are known as fleshy fruits. But pods, nut husks, clusters, and winged seeds (called keys) are also fruits because they contain the tree's seeds. These are called dry fruits.

On some fruits (such as peaches or plums), the part you eat surrounds the seed or seeds. But on other fruits (like walnuts and coconuts), the inner seed itself, the part we call the nutmeat, is good to eat.

PART II

All About Trees and Leaves

What Is a Tree?

Trees are amazing. They are the largest and oldest living things on Earth. Trees provide much of the oxygen that all living creatures must have to live.

More than twenty thousand different kinds of trees grow around the world—in the rain forests of the Amazon, in the craters of extinct volcanoes in Africa, on the streets of your neighborhood. What is it that makes trees unique in the plant kingdom?

Trees differ from all other plants because they are so big (usually over twelve feet tall) and so strong (with a single main stem, called a trunk, which is made out of wood), and because they live so long (many for hundreds of years).

When you see trees standing silently, you might not imagine there is a frenzy of activity going on inside them. But all day long, each part of a tree is busy working.

The Roots

Unless a tree is upended by a storm, you never get to see its remarkable maze of underground roots. Huge anchoring roots support the tree, reaching deep into the earth and sideways at least as wide as the branches grow, along with a network of medium-size roots. Otherwise, trees would crash down during storms and high winds.

The smaller, delicate feeder roots push out sideways from the bigger roots and are covered with tiny root hairs. These stay close to the surface to feed on the rich topsoil, absorbing the water and minerals the tree must have in order to produce food and grow.

> Large trees can transport 100 gallons of water per day from their roots to their branches.

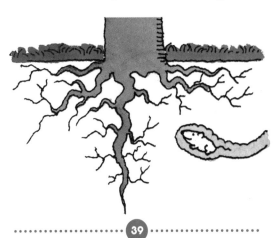

The Trunk

The trunk is made up of separate layers, and each layer has its own job to do.

The tough outer layer is the **bark**. Its job is to protect the tree. The bark keeps the tree cool in summer and warm in winter, stops the tree from losing too much water, and guards it from insects, fire, and disease.

The spongy inner bark, or **phloem**, is a highway for food. Sugar sap, made by the leaves, travels *down* the inner bark to feed the twigs, branches, trunk, and roots. Eventually, old inner bark becomes outer bark.

> **W**hich is bigger: a tree or the roots underneath the tree? The root system that anchors the tree is often bigger than the tree above it.

Although the green **cambium** layer is thinner than a piece of paper, it is one of the most important parts of the tree because it is in charge of making new inner bark and new sapwood. This is how the trunk grows wider.

The **sapwood**, or **xylem**, is the tree's second highway. This is the road for water and minerals (called root sap) to

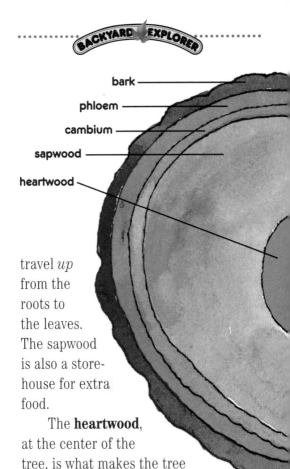

bark

phloem

cambium

sapwood

heartwood

travel *up* from the roots to the leaves. The sapwood is also a store-house for extra food.

The **heartwood**, at the center of the tree, is what makes the tree strong and rigid.

The Crown

The crown of a tree includes many of the things that make a tree look beautiful—the branches, twigs, leaves, flowers, and fruit. The crown has two main jobs—to make food for the tree and to make seeds. The leaves make food. The flowers and fruit make and protect the seeds, which will become new trees.

TWO KINDS OF TREES

Trees are divided into two major categories: coniferous and broadleaf.

Conifers carry their seeds in cones. Most conifers have needle-shaped or scaly leaves and most are evergreen. Evergreen trees, such as pines and spruces, keep their leaves all year long, even during winter.

Broadleaf trees have larger leaves than conifers. Most, but not all, are deciduous. Broadleaf deciduous trees, such as oaks, maples, and birches, lose their leaves in autumn, remain leafless through the winter, and grow new leaves in spring.

Nonconformists

Even in nature, there are exceptions to the rule. Here are two: **Deciduous conifers** (such as the tamarack) lose their leaves in autumn. **Broadleaf evergreens** (such as the live oak) keep their wide, flat leaves year-round.

How Trees Grow

Leaves are the first thing people associate with trees. Leaves are a tree's food factory. They make **sugar sap**, the tree's food, out of **root sap** (water and minerals), carbon dioxide (from the air), and sunshine with the help of a green chemical called **chlorophyll.** Chlorophyll is what makes leaves green. This food-manufacturing process is called **photosynthesis**.

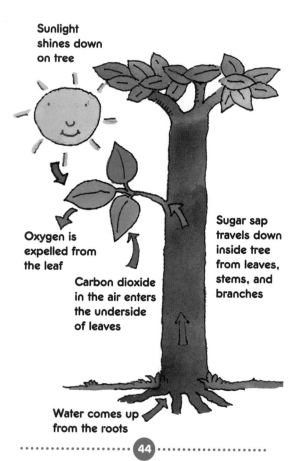

Sunlight shines down on tree

Oxygen is expelled from the leaf

Carbon dioxide in the air enters the underside of leaves

Sugar sap travels down inside tree from leaves, stems, and branches

Water comes up from the roots

Why Deciduous Trees Have Big Leaves

Most deciduous trees have big leaves because the leaves have to make enough food in six months to last the tree all year long. The bigger the leaf, the more sunshine it can absorb and the more food it can make.

When a deciduous tree loses its leaves in autumn, it lives on the food stored in the trunk and branches. During winter, the tree slows down a lot and doesn't use much food. But when spring comes, a tree needs lots of food for its new buds.

The Parts of a Leaf

Stem: The leaf stem attaches the leaf to its twig. Stand underneath a leafy tree and look up. Leaves are arranged on a branch so that each one gets some sun. Sunlight is so important for making food that if one leaf blocks all the light from another, the shaded leaf will turn yellow and die. Notice that the leaf

stems are different lengths—shorter or longer stems find their leaf a place in the sun.

The leaf stem is the pipeline through which root sap and sugar sap travel in and out of the leaf. It is flexible so that during a storm the leaf can flap back and forth like a kite on a string.

Veins: The lacy veins are the leaf's skeleton. They stiffen the leaf so its surface is exposed to sunlight. Veins look delicate, but they are the mini-tubes through which root sap and sugar sap travel in and out of the leaf.

Surface: The outer skin of a leaf is waterproof. Many leaves also have a waxy coating. This coating stops the leaf from losing too much water and also helps protect the leaf from insects.

Pores: Every leaf has hundreds of thousands of tiny pores, or stomata, through which it breathes. Most are on the bottom side of the leaf. Leaves take in air through these pores, using the carbon dioxide for photosynthesis; then they release oxygen and water vapor into the atmosphere, and draw up more water from the roots. You can't see it, but a tree is breathing out water vapor all day long.

Hairs: There are also tiny hairs on many leaves—you can actually feel fuzz on some leaves. The hairs protect the leaf from insects and drying winds, and also keep rainwater from coating the surface, which would prevent the pores from breathing.

Drip tips: Pointy leaf tips and lobes help rainwater run off a leaf more quickly.

LONG-DISTANCE FLIGHTS

Just because a leaf is lying on the ground under a tree doesn't mean it came from that tree. The wind blows leaves away from their trees, mixing them up like someone shuffling a deck of cards. In early autumn, take a handful of leaves from under a tree and try to identify which trees they came from. You might be surprised at how far some of them traveled!

Evergreen Leaves: Tough Guys

Winter cold doesn't kill narrow evergreen leaves because they are much tougher than the delicate leaves that grow on deciduous broadleaf trees.

Skinny evergreen needles don't rip in the wind, and snow slides off them. Also, a thick layer of wax coats each needle, preventing it from losing too much of the precious water inside and drying out.

Each evergreen needle has only one or two veins, which run down the center of the leaf and transport root sap and sugar sap into and out of the leaf.

Trees help conserve energy for your family by shading your home in the summer and creating a windbreak in the winter. Trees are also good noise barriers, making cities and neighborhoods quieter.

Evergreen leaves can't make as much food as the large broad leaves do, but they don't have to. Evergreen leaves don't fall off in autumn, so they continue to make food throughout the year—even on freezing days, when everything works in slow motion.

Evergreen trees can grow in places where broadleaf trees have a hard time surviving—the freezing Arctic, wind-swept mountains, and furnace-hot deserts.

THE PALM TREE

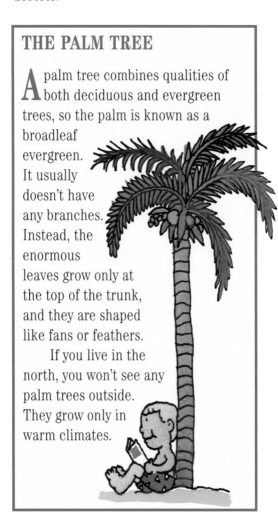

A palm tree combines qualities of both deciduous and evergreen trees, so the palm is known as a broadleaf evergreen. It usually doesn't have any branches. Instead, the enormous leaves grow only at the top of the trunk, and they are shaped like fans or feathers.

If you live in the north, you won't see any palm trees outside. They grow only in warm climates.

A Deciduous Tree Through the Seasons

Winter: Look for buds

In winter, the deciduous tree lies dormant. Its growth slows down, its food manufacturing activities grind almost to a halt, its roots almost stop drawing water from the earth, and its branches are bare and seemingly lifeless. But deep within the buds, the leaves are already growing and beginning to swell, protected by hard, overlapping scales.

Spring: Watch flowers and leaves bloom

As spring nears, the air warms, the ground thaws, the tree reawakens. Sap rises through its trunk. The buds burst open to reveal tiny, delicate flowers or leaves.

Some flowers have petals; others have drooping tails called catkins. Flowers that are fertilized swell to become fruits, bearing the seeds inside. Seeds that fell to the ground last autumn take root and their stems reach for light.

Summer: Look for fruits

In summer, as the seeds develop and the fruits mature, the flowers dry up and fall off. Tiny buds appear—these will lie dormant until next spring approaches. As summer ends, fruits of all kinds ripen—berries, nuts, pods. Within each of them are seeds, and each seed contains all the parts it needs to make a new tree.

Autumn: Collect fruits and seeds

As autumn comes, the ripe fruits and seeds fall to the ground. The leaves turn color and they also fall. The life of the tree once again slows—until springtime and the beginning of a new cycle.

Why Leaves Turn Color

As summer ends, the days get shorter and the weather gets cold. Deciduous trees know that now it is time for them to shed their leaves.

The green chlorophyll in the leaves disappears. All along, there were other colors in the leaves, but there was so much chlorophyll you couldn't see them. Now they have their chance. Leaves turn red, orange, yellow, purple, and brown.

Deciduous trees have good reason to shed their leaves. Leaves use up great quantities of water—without leaves a tree doesn't need nearly as much. When water in the ground freezes, the roots can no longer suck it up, but the leafless tree can live on water it has stored and won't die of thirst.

As leaves change color, a corky layer forms where the stem of each leaf is attached to the twig. Now nothing can get into or out of the leaves, and soon they break off and fall to the ground.

HOW SEEDS TRAVEL

To grow into new trees, seedlings must have plenty of sunlight, water, and minerals. If they stayed under the parent tree, they would be too crowded; also the parent tree's crown would shade them from the sun, and its enormous roots would use up most of the water and minerals in the soil. To survive, the ripe seeds must travel away from the parent tree.

Some seeds are carried away by animals either in the fruits or nuts they eat or bury (and sometimes forget about) or on their fur. Some seeds travel by wind or water to new rooting ground, and some seeds are scattered when the fruits carrying them pop open and shoot them out.

PART III

Some Common Trees

(And How to Tell Them Apart)

I t's very likely some of the following trees are growing somewhere near you. In fact, you may have found a leaf belonging to one of these trees on your Leaf Hunt. Just look for the leaf shape and see!

 Smooth-edged simple leaf

Catalpa (Indian bean tree):
Heart-shaped leaves and long pods (more than a foot long).

Redbud: Heart-shaped leaves and short pods (about three inches long).

Dogwood: Oval leaves with arched veins. White or pink flowers bloom in late spring.

Osage orange: Oval leaves, short thorns on the branches, and a yellow-green fruit (known as a hedge apple) about the size of a grapefruit.

Magnolia: Long, broad leaves and beautiful, fragrant flowers.

Pawpaw: Long, broad leaves and fruit shaped like a big lima bean.

 Toothed simple leaf

Poplar family (aspen, poplar, and cottonwood): Triangular or oval leaves on long leaf stalks. The leaves quiver in the slightest breeze. Catkins ripen into fluffy white seeds that blow around like falling snow.

Lombardy Poplar

*Balm of Gilead
(Ontario Poplar)*

Birch: Oval leaves and peeling
bark or bark with
black markings.

Paper Birch

Weeping willow: Long, skinny leaves
with tiny teeth.

Hackberry: Oval leaves that usually
have more teeth
above the middle
than below.
The bark of the
Hackberry has
corky warts.

Chestnut: Long, narrow leaves and a
spiny-husked nut.

Beech: Long, oval leaves with wavy edges and a spiny-husked nut.

Hand-shaped simple leaf

Maples: Hand-shaped leaves and double-winged seeds.

Silver Maple

Japanese Maple

Sugar Maple

Moosewood: A maple with white stripes on its bark.

Sycamore (plane tree): Hand-shaped leaf and bark that is camouflage-patterned.

Sweet gum: Hand-shaped leaf and a spiky seed ball.

Hand-shaped compound leaf

Hop tree: Three leaflets.

Ohio buckeye: Five or more long leaflets.

Horse chestnut: Five or more long leaflets that bulge near the end of each tapered tip.

Feather-shaped simple leaf

Oaks: Leaves usually shaped like jagged feathers. One thing all oaks have in common is that they grow acorns.

White Oak

Black Oak

Bur Oak

Feather-shaped compound leaf

Ash: Opposite leaves and single-winged seeds that look like canoe paddles.

White Ash

Honey locust: Bipinnate leaves, big thorns on the branches, and seed pods.

Shagbark hickory: Oval leaflets, peeling bark, and a smooth-husked nut.

Black walnut: Oval leaflets, rough dark-gray bark, and smooth-husked nut.

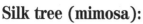

Silk tree (mimosa): Bipinnate leaves, rows of small leaflets, and a purple-and-white flower.

Cluster needles

Beach pine: Often found along the Pacific Coast, its needles grow in pairs and its cone is small and egg-shaped.

Jeffrey pine: Its long needles grow in clusters of three, and its cone can grow to twelve inches long.

Scotch pine: Its twisty needles grow in pairs, and its cone is usually about three inches long.

Western yellow pine: Its long needles grow in clusters of three, and its cone grows to about four inches long.

White pine: Long, soft needles that grow in clusters of five.

Tamarack (American larch):
Short deciduous needles (they drop off in winter) that grow in clusters of more than five.

Single needles

Hemlock: Its needles are flat and grow opposite each other.

Black spruce: It has the smallest cone of all the spruces, growing to about an inch and a half long.

Yew (taxus): It has needles like a conifer but it doesn't have cones. Instead, the tree grows round, red berries.

Douglas fir: Its needles are rounded and there are three-pronged bracts (leaflike structures) growing between the cone scales.

Scaly leaves

Arborvitae (white cedar):

Its leaves are yellow-green on top and paler underneath.

Common juniper: Its leaves are prickly and shiny green with a strip of white.

Rocky Mountain juniper: Its leaves look like very small scales and its berry-cone is tiny.

Three Special Finds

Sassafras: Its leaves may be shaped like a feather, a mitten, or a ghost saying boo.

Live oak: An evergreen that grows acorns. Its leaves may be smooth, spiny, or lobed.

American holly: Look for its distinctive spiny leaf.

Many universities and colleges have Web sites that include leaf identification keys for trees common in your state or area. Check online to see if there is one specifically for your backyard!

PART IV

Projects

- How much water evaporates from a leaf in a week?

- What's inside a gall?

- Which comes first in the spring—flowers or leaves?

- What happens to the billions of dead leaves and twigs?

- Why do cones close up tight when it rains?

You will discover the answers to these and other fascinating questions when you do the projects in this book. You will also learn how to create wonderful paintings, collages, and gifts from leaves, bark, dry fruit, and seeds. When you've gathered together a good collection of materials, you can keep busy doing projects all year long!

How to Press Leaves

Before you can mount leaves in your album or do many of the Backyard Explorer projects, you'll need to press the leaves you've collected to get the moisture out. Do this as soon as you get home or they'll curl up and be unusable. Here are two easy methods for pressing leaves: one takes two weeks but it's very, very easy; the other is super quick but you need adult supervision and some equipment.

Two-Week Method

Pat wet leaves dry, and cut off any thick stems. Lay leaves flat between four sheets of newspaper, making sure they don't touch each other. Add as many layers of leaves and newpapers to your pile as you wish.

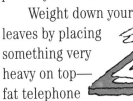

Weight down your leaves by placing something very heavy on top— fat telephone books are excellent. After about two weeks, carefully remove the leaves. They are now ready to mount in your album.

Store extra pressed leaves in a box so they won't get hurt.

Quick Method

Not everyone has the patience to wait two weeks for leaves to dry. Here is a quick way to press leaves, using an iron. You'll need the assistance of an adult.

Have an adult set up an ironing board and preheat a dry iron on the permanent press setting for two minutes.

Place a thin piece of cardboard on the ironing board, and cover it with a sheet of wax paper a little larger than your leaf. Place your leaf on top, cover it with another sheet of wax paper, and then a cotton rag, preferably smooth. A piece of an old sheet would be perfect.

Iron back and forth all over, making sure that each part of the leaf gets ironed for at least the count of 20. Remove the rag and cardboard. Carefully peel the wax paper from the leaf. Feel the leaf. It should be perfectly flat and have a slightly waxy surface, which will make it stronger. Now it is ready for mounting (see next page).

Stand the iron on its flat end when not in use. Always turn off and unplug the iron as soon as you are finished using it.

Mounting Leaves

After your leaves are pressed, you are ready to mount them on their album cards. If you wish, put reinforcements around the holes to strengthen them. Match the shape of your leaf to the correct album card. If you haven't already done so, make sure to cut off any thick stems. Paste or tape your leaf to its card.

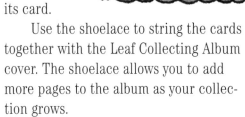

Use the shoelace to string the cards together with the Leaf Collecting Album cover. The shoelace allows you to add more pages to the album as your collection grows.

For cones, nuts, and other round things you collect, an egg carton or shoe box makes a great display case. A Christmas card box with see-through top is good for small things. But don't close the lids for several weeks. Your discoveries need air to dry out, so they won't get moldy. Once you have your collection sorted, cut and paste the album cards of the fruits and seeds in the box.

MAKING LEAVES
SHINY AND BRIGHT

When you apply decoupage glue to a leaf, it strengthens the leaf and makes it look shiny. You can buy the glue in an art supply store and use it to "paint" the mounted leaves on your album cards. Decoupage glue is easy to use. You can clean your brush and any spills with water.

Cover your work surface with newspaper. Dip your brush into the jar of decoupage glue and spread it evenly over the mounted leaf.

Let your cards dry overnight.

Growing Buds

When you look up at the buds in late winter and early spring, do you wonder what's inside? Are they flowers or leaves? Here's a chance to find out before everyone else does. You'll need an adult to help you collect some twigs.

1. In February, when buds are still tightly closed, have an adult help you cut off a 12-inch twig from several different kinds of trees. Use garden shears for a sharp, clean cut, and make the cuts at an angle. Never take more than you need. Make sure you take a twig from your favorite tree (see next page).

2. Fill a jar with water and put in the twigs. Place it on a sunny windowsill in a warm room. Change the water every few days.

3. Check your twigs daily, and notice how the buds begin to swell. Finally, the flower buds will burst open. Leaf buds will take a little more time.

Finding a Favorite Tree

One sunny spring day, take a walk and pick out your favorite broadleaf tree. Maybe you like the way its bark feels, or think the flowers are beautiful. Or maybe it grows outside your bedroom window, and you have known this tree for a long time.

Select a tree that is nearby and that has some low branches you can reach.

Throughout the year, observe what happens to your tree. In the spring, does it develop leaves or flowers first? What kind of leaves and fruit does it have? What colors do the leaves turn in autumn? Take pictures of your favorite tree in every season.

Find the album pages that say "Favorite Tree" on top. Put leaves and photographs of your tree on them. Mount extra photos on oaktag or colored paper. Write the date on each picture.

If your tree belongs to a neighbor, ask permission before you pick things from it.

A Secret Way to Identify Your Tree

If your favorite tree is in a park or on a city street, here's a secret way to identify it.

Find a big, unusual-looking stone and write your name on it with a black waterproof marking pen; then put the stone under your tree with the writing side facedown. No one will ever know that this is your special tree.

The Dead Leaf Mystery

Why aren't we up to our necks in old leaves? What happens to the billions of dead leaves in the woods? No one rakes them up. Somehow they disappear without our noticing. Bacteria, insects, and tiny animals turn the dead leaves back into soil and food for trees and plants. Would you like to see some of the members of this huge cleanup army?

1. Find a tree that has some rotting leaves and twigs beneath it. Scoop up some of the damp, loose soil underneath.

2. Lay newspaper on the ground outside and spread a very thin (quarter-inch-deep) layer of this soil on top.

3. Use a spoon or shovel to inspect the soil. Examine the pieces of rotting leaves, twigs, and nuts. You'll probably find plenty of bugs. Most of the meat eaters seem to rush around; the plant eaters move more slowly. Some spiders and centipedes are poisonous, so be very careful not to touch them.

4. See if you can find these plant eaters in the soil: snails, slugs, ants, grubs, millipedes.

5. Look for these meat eaters: spiders, false scorpions, centipedes, rove beetles.

6. See how many different kinds of insects and tiny animals you can find. Put each one in a small, clean jar (like a baby food jar) while you study it. When you're finished, let them go—they have a job to do.

Leafcards and Bookmarks

You can use leaves to make wonderful leaf postcards to send to your friends or bookmarks to give as gifts. You'll need: pencil, ruler, unlined index cards, postage stamps, scissors, clear contact paper, piece of cardboard, cellophane tape, and pressed leaves.

Leafcards

1. Cut a piece of clear contact paper slightly larger than the index card. Peel off the backing and lay the contact paper on the cardboard, sticky side up. Tape each corner down.

2. Choose pressed leaves that will look pretty on the index card—either one big leaf or several small leaves or evergreen needles. Place the leaves on the sticky sur-face of the contact paper. Cover them with the blank side of the index card and press down.

3. Remove the tape, turn the card over, and press your fingers around the edges of the leaves to get rid of air pockets.

4. Trim off the extra contact paper. Your leaf postcard is ready to mail.

5. Draw a line down the middle of the index card. On the left side, write a message to a friend; on the right, put a postage stamp and your friend's name and address.

Bookmarks

1. Draw a line down the middle of the long side of an index card, and cut it.

2. Using skinny broad leaves or evergreen needles, follow steps 2 to 4 (above). Leaf bookmarks make fun gifts that are also useful! If you like, write a short message on them such as "Happy Birthday!" or "I Love You, Mom!"

Capturing Water

Every day, the roots of a tree send up enormous amounts of water to the leaves. The leaves breathe it out through tiny holes, or pores, most of which are on the underside of the leaf.

You cannot see the water leaving because it is invisible—it has been turned into water vapor, which is a gas. But you can capture the vapor and turn it back into water.

1. On a hot summer day, put a small pebble in a plastic sandwich bag. Put the plastic bag over a small leaf that gets a lot of sunshine, and tie it tightly to the stem with a twist tie.

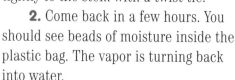

2. Come back in a few hours. You should see beads of moisture inside the plastic bag. The vapor is turning back into water.

3. Check each day to observe how much water is gathering in your bag. At the end of a week, carefully take off the bag. Use a measuring spoon to find out how much water is in the bag.

A small leaf that gets a lot of sun-

shine will give off about half a teaspoon of water in a week. Find out how much a big leaf will give off.

There are over 100,000 leaves on an average tree. Just think about how much water vapor trees send up into the air each day, especially in summer!

GIANT AIR CONDITIONERS

One big tree can have the cooling power of many air conditioners. A tree's crown makes shade, and its leaves give off moisture, which cools the air.

Hatching Leaf Galls

Leaf galls are insect homes found on leaves. Would you like to "hatch" the insect that lives inside?

1. In autumn, when the leaves are beginning to fall, look for bumpy galls on oak and willow leaves. There are hundreds of different kinds of galls, so you may find many different types—even on the same leaf. Galls can be as small as a pinhead or as big as a button.

2. Put leaves with galls in a jar.

Secure a small rag over the mouth of the jar with a rubber band. Keep the leaves damp and your jar outside in a place that's protected from rain. In early spring, the insects will come out. The insects that emerge may not be the ones who made the galls. Other insects attack galls, kill the first occupants, and take over their homes. When you have finished studying them, let the insects go.

Leaf Crowns

Leaf crowns are easy and fun to make, by yourself or with friends. And you can make them in the spring, summer, or autumn—depending on whether you want them to be green or brightly colored.

1. Collect large, fresh leaves with long stems (at least two to three inches). Don't use pressed leaves, because they might crack. Although fresh leaves don't last long, they will make a beautiful crown.

2. Cut off each stem close to the base of the leaf and set it aside.

3. Overlap two leaves the long way, vein side up, as shown. Where the two leaves overlap, make two small holes about one inch apart with the tip of a pencil. The holes should be big enough for a stem to fit through.

4. To pin two leaves together, take a stem and push it up through one set of holes. Then bend the stem and push it down through the other set of holes.

5. Now pin a third leaf to either leaf, again following the directions in

steps 3 and 4. Keep adding leaves until your crown is big enough to fit your head. Then pin the first leaf to the last leaf to make a circle.

6. For an extra fancy touch, decorate your crown with wildflowers. Carefully tuck the stem of each flower underneath a leaf stem pin.

7. If you make a crown with autumn leaves, you can gather bright leaves of many colors, or use just yellow leaves— then it will look like gold!

STAINED-GLASS LEAVES

Tape bright autumn leaves to your window. When sunlight shines through the leaves, you will be amazed at how beautiful they look.

Magic with Cones

Ripe brown cones close up tight when it's wet out in order to protect their seeds. If the seeds came out when it is raining, they would become wet and heavy and fall straight to the ground. In dry weather, their winged seeds can fly far away on a breeze and find a good place to grow.

Take an open brown cone, and sprinkle it with water. After about ten minutes you'll see it begin to close; in about an hour the scales will be shut. If you let it dry, the scales will open again in a few hours. Cones will open and shut whether they have seeds inside them or not.

This is an excellent magic trick to try on your friends: Secretly wet a cone before you show it to them, and then say you are "magically" going to make the cone close.

Leaf Art

Here are two different ways to make leaf paintings. Once they are dry, hang them on your wall, mount them in a scrapbook, or make notecards with them (simply fold a piece of paper in half and do your painting on either side).

Note: Autumn leaves are stiffer than green leaves and easier to handle for these projects.

WHAT YOU'LL NEED

Newspaper

Unpressed autumn leaves

Paintbrush

Poster paint in various colors

Colored construction paper or white paper

Leaf Prints

You can create a beautiful picture using leaves.

1. Cover a workspace with plenty of newspaper.

2 Choose several leaves with interesting shapes and vein patterns.

3. Use a brush or your fingers to paint the underside of each leaf (where the veins stick out) with poster paint.

4. Carefully pick up the wet leaf by

the stem and place it, paint side down, on a piece of colored construction paper or white paper.

5. Cover the leaf with another piece of paper and rub gently but firmly. Carefully take up the top piece of paper, then lift the leaf by its stem.

6. Repeat with several more leaves if you want, using different paint colors. To overlap leaf patterns, allow the first leaf print to dry before doing the next one.

Leaf Silhouettes

This is a painting of just the outside edge of your leaf.

1. Spread plenty of newspaper on your work surface.

2. Choose a leaf with lots of lobes or big teeth.

3. Place the leaf on a piece of paper, and hold it down with one hand. Paint all around the leaf, from the edge of the leaf onto the paper, using short outward strokes.

4. Carefully lift the leaf by its stem. Let the painting dry.

Autumn Collage

Use colorful leaves, pods, seeds, and cones to make an autumn collage. Not everything has to be whole—this project works well even with bits and pieces of things you've collected.

WHAT YOU'LL NEED

Pencil

Cardboard, any size

Page from coloring book (optional)

White paste

*Pressed leaves, pods, seeds, cones—
    whole and pieces*

Decoupage glue (optional)

1. Make a drawing in pencil on your cardboard. It could be of a tree, butterfly, flower, or a scene of mountains and birds. Or cut out a picture from a coloring book and paste it onto your cardboard.

2. Spread some paste in one area and start arranging some of your tree collection. Work on one section at a time and try to get a good balance of leaves and seeds and whatever else you've collected. When you have finished, let your collage dry for two days.

3. You can paint your collage with decoupage glue to give it a shiny finish.

Bark Rubbing

Bark covers and protects the tree trunk. As a trunk grows wider, its bark stretches and cracks. The bark of each type of tree cracks in its own special way—some peels off, some splits, and some makes deep furrows. Make a bark rubbing of your favorite tree.

WHAT YOU'LL NEED

Masking tape

Piece of unlined paper

Fat crayon of any color

1. Tape a piece of paper to the trunk of a tree with an interesting bark pattern.

2. Remove the paper from the crayon. Rub the side of the crayon back and forth over the paper. Soon you will begin to see the pattern of the bark on your paper.

3. Make bark rubbings of trees with different kinds of bark. Find a trunk with smooth bark and another with very rough bark.

4. Tape a leaf from the tree onto your bark rubbing.

Leaf Pals

If you don't live in a climate where leaves turn brilliant colors in autumn, why not exchange leaves through the mail with a friend or relative who does? Leaves that grow near you may be hard for your leaf pal to find, too. Or speak to your teacher. It would be fun for your whole class to exchange leaves with children from a school in a different part of the country. Always press leaves before sending them to someone else, and mail them between layers of thin card-board for extra protection.